IT'S NEVER OVER
MOVIE REVIEW

**A Deep Dive into Jeff Buckley's Legacy: Uncovering the
Music, the Man, and the Team Behind the Documentary**

Torin Bellamy

Disclaimer

This publication is an independent work of critical analysis, commentary, and review related to film and media. All views, opinions, and conclusions expressed herein are solely those of the author and do not necessarily reflect the views of any production companies, filmmakers, distributors, or trademark owners referenced.

Trademarks, service marks, logos, and other intellectual property mentioned or depicted within this book are the property of their respective owners. Their inclusion is for identification and critique only and does not imply endorsement, sponsorship, or any formal relationship with the author or publisher.

This book is intended for educational and informational purposes only and complies with applicable "fair use" and "fair dealing" copyright laws. The author and publisher have made every effort to ensure accuracy and reliability; however, no warranty is provided, and neither the author nor publisher assumes liability for any loss, injury, or damages arising from the use of the information contained herein.

Readers are encouraged to independently verify facts and seek professional advice where appropriate. By using this book, readers agree to indemnify and hold harmless the author and publisher against any claims, liabilities, losses, or damages arising from their use of the content.

This publication is not intended to replace professional advice or constitute legal counsel.

TABLE OF CONTENT

Introduction: A Journey Through Jeff Buckley's Legacy

Jeff Buckley's life and career, though tragically short, left a lasting imprint on the music world. Known for his ethereal voice and innovative approach to songwriting, Buckley is considered one of the most unique and influential artists of the 1990s. His album *Grace* is often hailed as a masterpiece, and even decades after his untimely death in 1997, his music continues to inspire musicians and fans alike. The documentary *It's Never Over* takes us deep into the life and legacy of Jeff Buckley, offering an intimate exploration of the man behind the music.

Overview of the Movie

It's Never Over is not just another documentary about a musical icon; it's a deeply personal and emotional journey into the heart of Jeff Buckley's life. Directed by Amy Berg, the film uncovers previously unseen footage and interviews with key figures who knew Buckley best. What sets this documentary apart is its careful attention to both the artistic and personal facets of Buckley's story. The film highlights his music, his complex relationships, and his enduring influence on the music industry.

The documentary doesn't shy away from the darker aspects of Buckley's life, including his struggles with fame, self-identity, and emotional vulnerability. It draws from interviews with his mother, Mary Guibert, who has been a key figure in preserving his legacy, as well as friends and collaborators like Aimee Mann, Ben Harper, and his bandmates from his short-lived career. These insights, combined with archival footage, create a compelling portrait of a man who, despite his brief time in the spotlight, left a profound and lasting impact on music and culture.

Purpose and Scope of the Review Book

The purpose of this book is to provide a comprehensive and thoughtful analysis of *It's Never Over*, both as a documentary and as a tribute to Jeff Buckley's extraordinary legacy. This review aims to explore the film in depth, considering not only the factual content but also the emotional and artistic layers that make it unique. By delving into the movie's structure, cinematography, interviews, and the emotional core of Buckley's story, this book will offer readers an insightful guide that enhances their understanding of the documentary.

We will also examine how *It's Never Over* captures the essence of Buckley's artistry. The film is as much about the man as it is about his music, and this book will highlight how the documentary weaves these two aspects together. The book will cover the creative decisions made by the filmmakers, including the choice of cast, the integration of Buckley's rare footage, and the film's portrayal of Buckley's struggles and triumphs. In doing so, we aim to show how this documentary adds to the understanding of Buckley as an artist and person, offering a new lens through which to appreciate his music.

Why Jeff Buckley's Story Matters Today

In an age dominated by fleeting musical trends, Jeff Buckley's music has stood the test of time. His unique sound, blending folk, rock, and soul, continues to resonate with new generations of listeners. Yet, beyond his incredible voice and songwriting, Buckley's story is one of profound emotional depth. His music reflected his internal struggles, his search for meaning, his complicated relationships, and his experiences with love, loss, and fame. These themes, universal and timeless, are as relevant today as they were in the 1990s.

The documentary *It's Never Over* brings these struggles to the forefront, making Buckley's journey feel as personal to modern viewers as it did for those who lived through it. The film reminds us that Buckley was more than just a musician; he was an artist who poured his soul into every note, leaving behind a legacy that speaks to the human experience.

Additionally, Buckley's story highlights the fragility of fame and the toll it can take on an individual. His brief but impactful career is a reminder of how fleeting success can be, and yet how lasting the effect of one's work can be on others. As the documentary explores his rise to fame, his battle with the expectations placed upon him, and his tragic death, it invites us to reflect on our own relationship to success, fame, and personal identity.

For fans of his music, *It's Never Over* is a chance to better understand the man behind the melodies. For those unfamiliar with his work, the film serves as an introduction to an artist whose legacy continues to inspire. The story of Jeff Buckley is more than just a biographical tale, it is a meditation on the complexities of life, the emotional power of music, and the enduring nature of art.

Chapter 1: Setting the Stage – Jeff Buckley's Impact on Music

Jeff Buckley was a once-in-a-generation talent whose influence on music cannot be overstated. Though his career was tragically short-lived, the work he left behind, especially his 1994 album *Grace*, continues to resonate with artists and fans alike. This chapter sets the stage for understanding Buckley's impact, both on the music world and on the film *It's Never Over*. His life and music serve as the emotional and artistic foundation of the documentary, exploring not only his genius but also the complex emotional landscape he inhabited.

Buckley's Life and Music: The Foundation of the Film

Jeff Buckley's life story is as intricate and captivating as the music he created. Born in 1966 to Mary Guibert, a classical pianist, and Tim Buckley, a folk musician who passed away when Jeff was only eight, Jeff was no stranger to the complexities of music and personal loss. His early exposure to music, coupled with the absence of his father, shaped his emotional and artistic growth. He inherited his father's musical talent but also carried the weight of the unresolved legacy his father left behind. This duality would become a recurring theme in his life and work.

Buckley's music was a blend of genres, incorporating elements of rock, folk, jazz, and blues. His vocal range, often compared to that of legendary artists like Freddie Mercury and Robert Plant, allowed him to explore various musical landscapes with ease and emotional depth. The documentary *It's Never Over* highlights his journey as a musician, from his early days performing in New York clubs to his rise to fame with *Grace*. The film doesn't just recount his musical achievements; it offers an intimate look at the emotional undercurrent of his work. Interviews with his mother, Mary Guibert, and those who were closest to him help provide context to the emotional weight behind his music.

The film opens with a portrayal of Buckley's early influences, how artists like Leonard Cohen, Van Morrison, and Jeff Buckley's own father, Tim, shaped his sound. The documentary's inclusion of archival footage and interviews with people who were with Buckley during this time, such as his bandmates Michael Tighe and Parker Kindred, provides an authentic and personal perspective on his development as an artist. These interviews highlight how Buckley was not only influenced by his father's music but also how his father's tragic and tumultuous life informed Buckley's approach to his own art.

The Legacy of *Grace* and the Cult Status of Jeff Buckley

At the heart of *It's Never Over* lies Buckley's masterpiece, *Grace*. Released in 1994, *Grace* remains an iconic record, one that critics still regard as one of the greatest albums of the 1990s. It was an album that captured both the fragility and the intensity of Buckley's artistry, blending haunting melodies with powerful lyrics that resonated on a deeply personal level. The documentary emphasizes *Grace* as the album that defined Buckley's legacy. The film doesn't shy away from the struggles and challenges he faced in recording the album, such as his self-doubt and fears of failure. It also shines a light on his passion and commitment to creating something timeless.

One of the most poignant aspects of *It's Never Over* is how it highlights the album's enduring impact, even in the years following Buckley's untimely death. Despite his passing, *Grace* found a new audience and continued to influence generations of musicians, from contemporary singer-songwriters to rock bands. The documentary captures the reverence that artists like Aimee Mann, who appears in the film, and Ben Harper have for Buckley's work. These interviews illustrate the profound effect Buckley's music has had on musicians across various genres.

The cult status of Jeff Buckley is a theme that runs throughout the film. Despite his relatively brief career, his influence only grew after his death in 1997, when he drowned in the Wolf River. Buckley became a tragic figure in the music world, a brilliant, enigmatic artist whose potential was cut short. Yet, his music lived on, and *Grace* became an album that is still celebrated and dissected by music lovers and critics alike. *It's Never Over* explores how Buckley's untimely death contributed to the mystique surrounding him, turning him into a legend.

Through archival footage, the documentary showcases Buckley's final performances and the impact they had on audiences. The film's exploration of his relationship with his fans, along with interviews from those who saw him perform, captures the magnetic energy that Buckley exuded on stage. His ability to connect with an audience, to move them with the raw emotion of his voice and lyrics, is a central theme in the documentary, and it's clear that *Grace* was just the beginning of what would have been an even greater musical journey.

Understanding Buckley's Musical Genius Through the Lens of Film

What makes Jeff Buckley's music stand out is not just his vocal talent or his songwriting ability but his emotional honesty. His songs often dealt with themes of love, loss, and existential longing, and his ability to convey these emotions through music was unparalleled. The documentary *It's Never Over* takes us behind the scenes of Buckley's creative process, offering insight into how he crafted his music and the emotional experiences that inspired it.

The film takes a closer look at the making of *Grace*, examining how Buckley meticulously shaped each track. Interviews with his bandmates, such as Michael Tighe and Parker Kindred, provide a glimpse into the collaborative process behind the album. The documentary also touches on Buckley's love for improvisation, as seen in the recording of *Grace* and during his live performances. His ability to reinterpret his own songs on stage, often making them feel raw and new, is a testament to his artistic genius.

The documentary also delves into the unique blend of influences that shaped Buckley's sound. While his father's folk background played a significant role, Buckley also embraced other genres like jazz, blues, and rock, which gave his music a timeless quality. *It's Never Over* emphasizes how Buckley's genre-blending style allowed him to transcend the boundaries of any one musical category, making his work more accessible and relevant to listeners across generations.

Finally, the documentary explores how Buckley's vulnerability and openness in his music set him apart from other artists of his time. His willingness to express his deepest fears, desires, and heartbreaks made his music not only relatable but also profoundly human. His ability to capture the universal experiences of love, longing, and loss resonated with listeners on a deeply emotional level. Through the lens of *It's Never Over*, we gain a greater appreciation for how Buckley's vulnerability informed his music, transforming him into a voice for those who felt unheard and misunderstood.

Chapter 2: A Closer Look at the Documentary

It's Never Over is a poignant, intimate documentary that not only chronicles the life of Jeff Buckley but also reflects on the complex emotional and artistic journey that defined his short but impactful career. Directed by Amy Berg, this film takes an unflinching look at the artist's life through archival footage, interviews with key figures, and raw glimpses into Buckley's personal and professional struggles. In this chapter, we take a closer look at the film, its themes, and the way the story of Jeff Buckley's legacy is told.

Overview of *It's Never Over*

It's Never Over is more than just a typical biographical documentary. While it certainly paints a comprehensive picture of Jeff Buckley's life, from his early influences to his rise to fame, it also delves into the deeper emotional terrain of the artist, his relationships, and his hauntingly beautiful music. The film does not simply focus on his achievements or his tragic death; it reveals the internal battles he faced and the emotional vulnerability he often tried to conceal.

The documentary's structure is designed to evoke a sense of intimacy and immediacy with Buckley, as if the viewer is sitting in the room with the people who knew him best. It features rare interviews with those closest to him, including his mother, Mary Guibert, who is one of the documentary's central figures. Guibert's perspective offers invaluable insight into Buckley's personality and the complexities of their mother-son relationship. The film also includes conversations with his bandmates, such as Michael Tighe and Parker Kindred, as well as musicians like Aimee Mann and Ben Harper, who speak about Buckley's influence on their own work.

The documentary also gives voice to archival footage of Buckley, showcasing his live performances and candid moments that allow the audience to experience the artist's vulnerability firsthand. These raw and unfiltered moments allow the viewers to connect with the essence of Jeff Buckley as a person and an artist, making his story feel even more profound.

Ultimately, *It's Never Over* is a film that honors the legacy of a man whose voice and music transcended time, all the while acknowledging the complexities of his life that contributed to the brilliance of his work. It is a testament to his artistic spirit and the emotional depth he brought to his music, showing us not only the artist but the human being behind the voice.

Key Themes and Messages Explored in the Film

Throughout *It's Never Over*, several key themes emerge that reflect the complexity of Jeff Buckley's life and music. These themes are deeply woven into the fabric of the documentary, providing viewers with a comprehensive understanding of the man behind the music.

1. **Artistic Struggle and Identity**
   One of the primary themes of the documentary is

Buckley's ongoing struggle with his identity as an artist. Interviews with Mary Guibert and those who worked closely with Buckley reveal his constant battle with self-doubt, imposter syndrome, and the pressure to live up to the legacy of his father, Tim Buckley. This theme is explored in depth through the use of archival footage that shows Buckley grappling with his own potential and the emotional cost of fame. His vulnerability is laid bare, as the film doesn't shy away from showing how these internal struggles informed the music he created.

2. **The Burden of Legacy**

The shadow of his father's legacy loomed large over Buckley's career, and the documentary delves into the emotional complexity of this relationship. Tim Buckley was a folk artist with a cult following, and although Jeff inherited his father's musical gifts, he had to contend with the expectations placed upon him. The film explores this in interviews with Mary Guibert, who sheds light on her own experiences as a mother and the challenges she faced in helping Jeff navigate his own path without being overshadowed by his father's fame.

3. **Love, Loss, and Vulnerability**
Buckley's music often touched on themes of love, heartbreak, and personal loss. *It's Never Over* reflects this emotional core through interviews with his bandmates and romantic partners, such as Rebecca Moore and Joan Wasser (later known as the musician Joan As Police Woman). Their reflections on their time with Buckley reveal a man who, despite his public persona as a confident performer, was deeply sensitive and vulnerable. The documentary explores how his love life and relationships influenced the songs on *Grace*, with tracks like "Lover, You Should've Come Over" being cited as reflections of his emotional turmoil.

4. **The Legacy of *Grace* and the Cult of Jeff Buckley**
Another central theme of the documentary is the enduring legacy of *Grace* and its place in the music world. Despite Buckley's untimely death, his music continued to inspire new generations. Through interviews with musicians like Aimee Mann and Ben Harper, the film shows how *Grace* influenced their work and how it became a cult album in the years following its release. The film emphasizes how Buckley's voice and

songwriting style set him apart from other artists of his time, and how his music continues to resonate with audiences today.

Structure of the Documentary: How the Story Unfolds

The structure of *It's Never Over* is carefully designed to guide the viewer through Jeff Buckley's life, music, and emotional journey. Rather than following a strict chronological order, the documentary intertwines moments from Buckley's personal life with footage of his performances and interviews with those who knew him best. This approach allows the film to focus more on the emotional and artistic journey of Buckley, rather than simply recounting the events of his life.

The documentary opens with a reflection on Buckley's early years, setting the stage for his rise to fame. We hear from his mother, Mary Guibert, who discusses his childhood and the early influences that shaped him. This provides essential context for understanding Buckley's internal conflict and his struggles to find his own artistic voice while dealing with the pressures of being the son of a famous musician.

As the film progresses, it moves into Buckley's time in New York, where he began to find his footing as a musician. Through interviews with bandmates like Michael Tighe and Parker Kindred, the documentary explores the formation of his sound and the dynamics of the group that helped bring his music to life. These discussions are interspersed with archival footage from his live performances, which showcase Buckley's magnetic stage presence and his ability to captivate an audience with nothing but his voice and guitar.

The film's pacing slows down in moments of reflection, allowing the viewer to feel the emotional weight of Buckley's personal struggles. We see how his relationship with his father, his lovers, and his own sense of self shaped the songs that would become *Grace*. As the documentary nears its conclusion, it focuses on the lasting impact of *Grace* and how Buckley's death, while tragic, only further cemented his place in the pantheon of great musical artists.

The structure of *It's Never Over* allows the viewer to feel not only the highs of Buckley's success but also the lows of his personal and emotional battles. It is a documentary that balances artistry with vulnerability, and by the end, the viewer comes away with a deep understanding of who Jeff Buckley was, both as a person and as a musical icon.

Chapter 3: Behind the Lens – The Making of the Documentary

Creating a documentary about a figure as influential and enigmatic as Jeff Buckley is no small feat. It requires a deep understanding of the subject, a team of creative visionaries, and access to rare archives and never-before-seen footage to truly capture the essence of the artist. *It's Never Over* is not just a film about Buckley's life, it's a cinematic exploration of his emotional journey, his artistic genius, and the people who knew him best. In this chapter, we delve into the behind-the-scenes process of making the documentary, from the directors and producers to the challenges they faced during production.

The Visionaries: Directors, Producers, and the Creative Team

At the heart of *It's Never Over* is the vision of director Amy Berg, a filmmaker known for her work on documentaries that dive deep into the human experience. Berg's ability to balance sensitive material with artistic storytelling made her the ideal choice to bring Buckley's story to life on the screen. Her previous works, such as *Deliver Us from Evil* and *West of Memphis*, demonstrate her knack for handling complex subjects with a compassionate and nuanced approach.

Berg's vision for *It's Never Over* was to create a film that was both intimate and insightful, one that showcased not only Buckley's musical brilliance but also the emotional depth of his life. She carefully selected a team of producers and cinematographers who shared her passion for capturing the rawness of Buckley's story. Producers like Rachel Miller and Aaron L. Gilbert helped to bring the film to fruition, ensuring that it was both a respectful tribute and a compelling cinematic experience. Their experience in working on high-profile documentaries gave them the expertise needed to tackle the sensitive nature of Buckley's life and legacy.

The film's creative team, including the editors, sound designers, and cinematographers, worked tirelessly to create a cohesive narrative that felt both personal and universal. Cinematographer John Churchman's contribution was particularly notable, as he used lighting and camera work to create a mood that mirrored the emotional tone of Buckley's music, fragile, haunting, and intimate. The editing team, led by Sharon O'Rourke, made sure that the narrative flowed seamlessly, allowing the documentary to build a deeper connection with the audience as it delved into Buckley's journey.

Together, this team of visionaries worked not just to document Buckley's life but to bring his spirit into the film, capturing the essence of who he was as a person and as an artist. The careful thought and dedication behind the direction and production of *It's Never Over* is evident throughout the documentary, making it a fitting tribute to the legacy of Jeff Buckley.

Filming Locations, Archives, and the Use of Rare Footage

One of the key elements that sets *It's Never Over* apart from other music documentaries is its use of rare and previously unreleased footage of Jeff Buckley. The film makes excellent use of archival materials, live performance videos, behind-the-scenes footage, and personal recordings, that help to humanize Buckley and offer the audience a glimpse into his world. The team was fortunate enough to access never-before-seen video of Buckley performing at small venues and rehearsing with his band, providing an intimate portrait of his artistry.

Filming locations played a critical role in capturing the essence of Buckley's life and work. The documentary takes viewers to key locations that were integral to his artistic journey, including the iconic Sin-é Café in New York City, where Buckley performed early in his career. The film features rare footage of Buckley onstage at Sin-é, capturing the raw energy and vulnerability he exhibited during these formative years. The location itself, an intimate, no-frills venue, was a place where Buckley truly honed his craft, and the documentary's inclusion of this footage helps to convey the significance of these early performances in shaping his sound.

In addition to the Sin-é performances, the film also makes use of archival interviews and photographs that provide insight into Buckley's personal life. Interviews with his mother, Mary Guibert, and close friends like Aimee Mann and Ben Harper offer a more personal perspective on his character. These archival materials not only highlight Buckley's musical talents but also his complex emotional world, shedding light on the man behind the music. Through these rare glimpses, the documentary allows viewers to understand Buckley not just as an artist but as a human being, filled with the same struggles and triumphs that anyone might face.

Challenges Faced During Production

Making a documentary about a beloved yet tragic figure like Jeff Buckley comes with its share of challenges, particularly when it comes to balancing the portrayal of his life's highs and lows. One of the key challenges the filmmakers faced during production was ensuring that the documentary felt authentic and true to Buckley's memory, without sensationalizing or exploiting the more difficult aspects of his life.

One of the most significant challenges was gaining access to the people closest to Buckley. Many of his family members, friends, and collaborators are protective of his legacy, and gaining their trust required a careful and respectful approach. Amy Berg and her team worked tirelessly to gain the cooperation of Mary Guibert, who is deeply involved in preserving her son's memory. Guibert's role in the documentary is crucial, as she provides much of the insight into Buckley's life, both as a mother and as an advocate for her son's legacy. Her willingness to participate and share her memories of Jeff was essential to the film's emotional depth.

Another challenge the filmmakers faced was navigating the complex and sometimes painful aspects of Buckley's life. His tragic death and the unresolved emotional issues that he faced in his personal life were key elements of the documentary, but the team had to handle these sensitive topics with care. In interviews with people like Aimee Mann and Parker Kindred, the film explores Buckley's struggles with fame, self-worth, and the impact of his father's legacy. These interviews are heartfelt and emotional, but the filmmakers made sure to respect the dignity of the people involved, allowing them to speak candidly without exploiting their personal pain.

Additionally, the team had to contend with the challenge of accurately portraying Buckley's music and artistry. His sound was incredibly unique, blending folk, rock, jazz, and blues, and translating that on screen in a way that captured the spirit of his music was no easy task. The team worked closely with sound designers to ensure that Buckley's music was presented in a way that allowed viewers to experience the raw emotion behind each note. Through careful sound editing and the use of live performance footage, the documentary successfully captures the feeling of Buckley's performances, allowing the audience to hear the soul-stirring intensity of his music.

Collaborations with Key Individuals in Buckley's Life

One of the most powerful aspects of *It's Never Over* is its focus on the relationships that shaped Jeff Buckley's life and music. The documentary features interviews with key individuals who knew Buckley intimately, including his mother, Mary Guibert, who was instrumental in helping to preserve his legacy after his death. Guibert's insights are invaluable, providing a window into Buckley's personality, his emotional struggles, and his creative process.

The film also includes reflections from Buckley's bandmates, such as Michael Tighe and Parker Kindred, who were instrumental in bringing *Grace* to life. Their interviews reveal the camaraderie and creative collaboration that defined Buckley's music, as well as the challenges they faced while working with such a unique and emotionally intense artist. Their stories offer a glimpse into the dynamic of Buckley's live performances, where his raw emotional energy and talent could transform a song in real time.

Additionally, musicians like Aimee Mann and Ben Harper speak to the influence that Buckley's music had on their own work. Their contributions to the documentary highlight the far-reaching impact of Buckley's sound, showing how his artistry continues to inspire musicians across genres. These collaborations with people who knew Buckley best serve as a powerful reminder of how much he meant to the people around him and to the music world as a whole.

Chapter 4: Cast, Interviews, and Real-Life Voices

The emotional heart of *It's Never Over* lies in the voices of those who knew Jeff Buckley the best: his family, friends, and collaborators. These real-life voices offer insight into the artist's complex personality, his relationships, and the emotional landscape that shaped his music. In this chapter, we take a closer look at the key individuals featured in the documentary and explore the profound impact their reflections have on our understanding of Buckley as a person and as an artist.

The Role of Mary Guibert and Family Insights

Perhaps the most significant and emotionally resonant voice in *It's Never Over* comes from Mary Guibert, Jeff Buckley's mother. Guibert's involvement in the documentary is crucial, as she not only sheds light on her son's childhood and early development but also offers an intimate and candid perspective on his struggles as an adult. As someone who worked tirelessly to preserve her son's legacy after his untimely death, Guibert's role in the film is pivotal in painting a more complete picture of Buckley's life.

Through her interviews, Guibert provides invaluable insights into Buckley's character, his sensitivity, his drive to succeed, and his emotional vulnerability. She speaks openly about their complicated relationship, which, like many mother-son relationships, was filled with love, conflict, and a deep understanding of one another. Guibert also reflects on the emotional toll of being the mother of such a talented yet troubled individual, describing how she navigated the challenges of supporting Buckley as an artist while simultaneously dealing with the inevitable pressures of fame and loss.

One of the most moving aspects of her participation in the documentary is her willingness to discuss the pain of losing her son. Guibert doesn't shy away from the heartbreak of Jeff's death and the overwhelming grief that followed. However, she also speaks to the sense of pride she feels for the music and legacy he left behind. Her reflections help the audience understand Buckley not only as an artist but also as a son, whose personal struggles were closely tied to the music he created. In this sense, Guibert's voice is a critical lens through which we come to understand the emotional depth and complexity of Jeff Buckley's life.

Contributions from Fellow Musicians: Aimee Mann, Ben Harper, and Others

In addition to Mary Guibert, *It's Never Over* features interviews with some of the most influential musicians who were personally affected by Jeff Buckley's music. Aimee Mann and Ben Harper, two renowned musicians whose work shares Buckley's emotional depth, offer profound reflections on the ways in which Buckley's artistry shaped their own careers.

Aimee Mann, known for her introspective songwriting and emotionally raw performances, speaks to the power of Buckley's voice and the profound impact it had on her own creative process. Mann and Buckley shared a unique connection, both artists were deeply invested in exploring the emotional complexities of life, love, and loss through their music. In her interview, Mann discusses how she felt a deep kinship with Buckley, despite their different musical styles. She credits his ability to blend raw emotion with technical precision as one of the reasons why his music resonates so deeply with listeners. Her interview also touches on their brief but meaningful friendship, giving the audience a glimpse into the personal side of Buckley that few people were able to see.

Ben Harper, another influential voice in the documentary, discusses how Buckley's music influenced his own work and how his artistry transcended genre. Harper, who is known for blending folk, blues, and rock, explains how Buckley's haunting renditions of classic songs, particularly his cover of Leonard Cohen's "Hallelujah," inspired him to take a more vulnerable approach to his own music. Harper's interview highlights the emotional power of Buckley's music, noting that Buckley had a way of making every performance feel like a personal experience, one that invited listeners into his inner world. For Harper, Buckley's influence was not just musical; it was deeply emotional and spiritual. His contribution to the documentary offers a rich, reflective insight into how Buckley's music continues to inspire musicians across genres.

Other musicians who contributed to the film include Joan Wasser (Joan As Police Woman), who had a close personal relationship with Buckley, and Michael Tighe, Buckley's bandmate and collaborator. These voices further enrich the documentary, providing a more comprehensive view of Buckley's impact on the music world and the people who were closest to him. Each of these musicians shares a unique perspective on Buckley's artistry, offering a multi-faceted view of his legacy.

Exploring the Interviews: Emotional and Introspective Reflections

One of the most striking elements of *It's Never Over* is the emotional and introspective nature of the interviews. Throughout the film, those closest to Buckley, including his bandmates, lovers, and family members, reflect on their personal connections with him, often with a deep sense of longing and vulnerability. These interviews allow the viewer to connect with the human side of Jeff Buckley, the side that was not always visible in his public persona as a rising rock star.

The interviewees in the documentary offer candid and sometimes painful reflections on Buckley's emotional struggles, his desire for connection, and his ongoing battle with self-doubt. His bandmates, for instance, recount how Buckley's intensity and perfectionism often created tension within the band, but also how his artistry inspired them to push the boundaries of their own musicianship. Michael Tighe and Parker Kindred, in particular, speak to the deep bond they shared with Buckley as creative collaborators. Their interviews capture the joy and frustration of working with an artist who was constantly striving for something more, someone who was both a genius and a deeply sensitive soul.

Joan Wasser, Buckley's romantic partner at the time of his death, offers an especially poignant perspective on their relationship. She recalls the emotional highs and lows of being with an artist who poured so much of himself into his music but often struggled with his own personal demons. Wasser's reflections offer a window into Buckley's internal world, highlighting the complexity of his character and the vulnerability he often tried to hide behind his music.

What makes these interviews so powerful is the honesty with which each individual speaks. There is no attempt to gloss over the difficulties of knowing Buckley or to sanitize his legacy. Instead, the interviews allow us to see the real Jeff Buckley, flawed, brilliant, conflicted, and deeply human. The candid nature of these reflections gives the documentary a raw emotional depth, allowing the viewer to understand Buckley's struggles not only through his music but through the eyes of those who loved him and were impacted by his presence.

The emotional weight of these interviews is not just about recounting Buckley's life but about understanding the profound effect he had on those around him. The way these individuals speak about him, whether in admiration, love, or sadness, creates an atmosphere of reflection that permeates the film. It's clear that Buckley's impact went beyond his music; he left an indelible mark on the people who knew him, and their stories bring an emotional richness to the documentary.

Chapter 5: Cinematic Elements – The Art of Documentary Filmmaking

The art of documentary filmmaking is not just about telling a story, it's about capturing the essence of a person, a time, and a place in such a way that the viewer feels deeply connected to the subject. In *It's Never Over*, Amy Berg and her creative team employed an array of cinematic elements to weave together the life of Jeff Buckley, portraying not only his music and legacy but also the complex emotions that defined his existence. From the cinematography to the role of music and the editing techniques, every aspect of the film works in harmony to evoke a powerful emotional response. This chapter takes a closer look at how these cinematic elements come together to tell Jeff Buckley's story.

Cinematography and Visual Style

The cinematography of *It's Never Over* plays a crucial role in setting the tone and atmosphere of the documentary. Cinematographer John Churchman, known for his ability to capture the emotional subtleties of a subject, crafted a visual style that enhances the intimate and reflective nature of the film. The camera work in *It's Never Over* is purposeful, focusing not just on the faces of the interviewees but also on the details that evoke a sense of time and place.

One of the standout features of the cinematography is the use of lighting and framing to create a mood that mirrors the emotional landscape of Jeff Buckley's life. For example, the film often utilizes soft lighting during reflective moments, highlighting the vulnerability of the subjects speaking about Buckley. In contrast, darker, more moody lighting is used during moments of tension or sorrow, reflecting the struggles that Buckley faced with fame, his identity, and personal relationships. The lighting serves as a visual metaphor for Buckley's inner turmoil and the complexities of his journey.

The documentary also makes effective use of archival footage, particularly from Buckley's early performances. These live concert shots are not only visually compelling but also offer a glimpse into the raw energy of Buckley's stage presence. The camera lingers on Buckley's expressions, capturing the intensity of his performance. This visual focus on Buckley's face during key moments on stage allows the viewer to connect with the depth of emotion he conveyed through his music. These moments are juxtaposed with shots of interviewees like Mary Guibert, Aimee Mann, and Michael Tighe, creating a visual rhythm that alternates between past and present, performance and reflection.

The color palette of the film also contributes to its emotional tone. The muted tones, sepia, grays, and soft blues, create a sense of nostalgia and melancholy, evoking the bittersweet nature of Buckley's short life. These visual choices enhance the film's ability to convey the emotional weight of the subject matter, making the audience feel as if they are not just observing Buckley's story but experiencing it alongside him.

Music's Role in the Documentary: A Soundtrack to Jeff Buckley's Story

Music is, of course, the heart and soul of *It's Never Over*. Jeff Buckley's songs are woven throughout the documentary, not only as a way of celebrating his artistry but also as a means of deepening the emotional connection between the viewer and the story. The film features several key tracks from Buckley's *Grace*, such as "Hallelujah," "Lover, You Should've Come Over," and "Last Goodbye," each of which plays a crucial role in expressing the themes of love, loss, and longing that pervade the film.

One of the most impactful moments in the documentary is the use of Buckley's haunting cover of Leonard Cohen's "Hallelujah." This song, often considered one of the defining tracks of Buckley's career, is given a prominent place in the documentary. The film uses this song not only to showcase Buckley's vocal brilliance but also to capture the emotional depth of his character. As the camera lingers on Buckley's expressive face during a live performance of "Hallelujah," the song serves as both a tribute to his artistry and a window into the complexities of his emotional world. The decision to feature this song so prominently in the documentary highlights how Buckley's music transcended mere performance; it was an expression of his soul.

Beyond his own music, the soundtrack of *It's Never Over* also includes contributions from artists who were influenced by Buckley, such as Aimee Mann and Ben Harper. These artists speak about the profound effect that Buckley's music had on their own work, and their contributions help to create a sense of continuity between Buckley's music and the broader musical landscape. The inclusion of these artists' reflections on Buckley's influence further underscores the film's central message: that Buckley's music, though tragically brief, left an indelible mark on the music world.

In addition to the music, the sound design of the film plays an essential role in setting the tone. The ambient soundscapes, such as the quiet rustling of leaves or the distant sounds of a city at night, are used to enhance the reflective mood of the documentary. The combination of Buckley's music and the subtle sound design immerses the viewer in the world of the film, making the emotional journey feel even more personal and immersive.

Editing Techniques and the Creation of Emotional Impact

The editing of *It's Never Over* is one of the film's most powerful elements. Sharon O'Rourke, the film's editor, carefully structured the documentary to create a seamless flow between Buckley's past and present, between his music and his personal life, and between interviews and archival footage. The pacing of the film is deliberate, allowing the viewer time to absorb the emotional weight of each moment while keeping the narrative moving forward.

One of the most effective editing techniques used in the documentary is the juxtaposition of live performance footage with interview segments. For instance, during a discussion about Buckley's stage presence, the documentary cuts to a performance of "Last Goodbye," showing the intensity and emotion with which Buckley approached each song. The transition from interview to performance allows the viewer to connect the personal reflections of Buckley's collaborators with the raw energy of his live performances. This contrast between the reflective, often somber tone of the interviews and the energy of the performances creates an emotional rhythm throughout the film, pulling the viewer into the emotional highs and lows of Buckley's life.

The documentary also uses subtle visual transitions, such as fading between archival footage and present-day interviews, to create a sense of continuity between the past and the present. These transitions serve as a visual metaphor for how Buckley's legacy continues to live on through his music and the people who were influenced by him. The editing style is clean and unobtrusive, allowing the emotional impact of the story to take center stage without being overshadowed by flashy effects or unnecessary embellishments.

Another key element of the editing is the use of silence and pause. The film often allows for moments of stillness, particularly during emotional interviews or reflections on Buckley's life. These pauses create a sense of space for the viewer to reflect on what has been said or shown, adding depth and gravity to the emotions being conveyed. This technique is particularly effective when paired with the music, allowing Buckley's songs to resonate even more deeply as they fill the silence.

Chapter 6: The Emotional Core – Buckley's Personal Struggles and Triumphs

The emotional core of *It's Never Over* is rooted in Jeff Buckley's personal struggles, his internal battles, and his triumphs, both in his music and in his life. While his incredible talent and his hauntingly beautiful music made him a musical icon, Buckley was also a man who faced profound emotional challenges. The documentary doesn't shy away from exploring these complexities. In fact, it's the rawness of his struggles and the depth of his triumphs that allow us to truly understand the man behind the music. This chapter takes a closer look at how *It's Never Over* delves into Buckley's vulnerability, the ways in which the documentary tackles his personal challenges, and how it uncovers the true essence of Buckley as a person.

Buckley's Vulnerability and the Complexity of His Character

One of the most powerful aspects of *It's Never Over* is its ability to show Jeff Buckley not just as a musician but as a human being, flawed, sensitive, and vulnerable. From the beginning, Buckley's vulnerability is evident in his music. His lyrics were often deeply introspective, touching on themes of love, loss, and longing. However, the documentary reveals that Buckley's vulnerability extended far beyond his music. Interviews with his mother, Mary Guibert, and close friends like Aimee Mann and Michael Tighe, offer a window into Buckley's personal life, shedding light on his struggles with self-doubt, emotional pain, and the pressure of living up to the legacy of his father, Tim Buckley.

Mary Guibert, in particular, speaks candidly about her son's inner conflicts. She describes him as a person who was always searching for something, whether it was validation, peace, or artistic fulfillment. Despite his outward success, Buckley struggled with feelings of inadequacy and the sense that he had yet to fully find his place in the world. Guibert reveals that Buckley often grappled with the idea of living in the shadow of his father, whose untimely death left a significant impact on his son's sense of identity. The film portrays Buckley as a man who was, in many ways, still searching for himself, a journey that is mirrored in the emotional intensity of his music.

Buckley's vulnerability also shines through in his relationships, especially with his lovers. Joan Wasser, who was romantically involved with Buckley during the final years of his life, offers an intimate and heartfelt perspective on their relationship. Wasser speaks about the emotional highs and lows of being with an artist who was constantly battling his inner demons, but she also highlights Buckley's tender, caring side. These conflicting aspects of his character, the sensitive artist and the tortured soul, are captured in the documentary, allowing the viewer to see the full scope of Buckley's complexity as a person.

The Documentary's Approach to His Struggles and Triumphs

It's Never Over doesn't attempt to sanitize Buckley's life or present him as a flawless hero. Instead, the documentary focuses on his internal struggles and the personal demons he faced, while also celebrating his triumphs as an artist. The film takes a balanced approach, showing how Buckley's vulnerability was both a source of pain and a wellspring of artistic inspiration.

One of the most compelling elements of the documentary is its exploration of Buckley's emotional struggles with fame. Interviews with his friends and collaborators paint a picture of a man who was ambivalent about his growing celebrity status. While he appreciated the recognition of his talent, Buckley was deeply uncomfortable with the attention that came with it. He often expressed feeling overwhelmed by the expectations placed on him, not only as an artist but also as the son of a legendary musician. The film delves into Buckley's fears of being defined solely by his father's legacy, showing how this fear fueled much of his emotional turmoil.

The documentary also explores Buckley's struggle with his own sense of identity. This is particularly evident in the way he grappled with his creative vision. He was constantly pushing himself to explore new musical territories, but at the same time, he struggled to find a sound that fully encapsulated who he was as an artist. His drive for perfectionism and his fear of failure are palpable throughout the documentary. The film's interviews with his bandmates, such as Michael Tighe and Parker Kindred, reveal how this pressure to succeed often led to moments of tension and frustration within the band. However, these moments of struggle also gave rise to some of the most powerful and emotionally resonant music of Buckley's career.

Despite these challenges, the documentary also highlights Buckley's triumphs, particularly his success with *Grace*. The album remains one of the most revered records of the 1990s, and the documentary emphasizes how it was a culmination of his emotional struggles and artistic ambitions. The film highlights key moments in the creation of *Grace*, including the recording process and Buckley's relentless pursuit of perfection. His willingness to lay bare his emotional vulnerability in his music became a defining feature of his work, and it is through this willingness to expose his inner world that *Grace* became such a timeless and influential album.

Uncovering the Person Behind the Music

It's Never Over is not just a documentary about Jeff Buckley the musician, it's a film that uncovers the person behind the music. The documentary's focus on Buckley's emotional journey, his relationships, and his internal struggles allows us to see the man behind the myth. While his music remains his lasting legacy, the documentary emphasizes that Buckley's humanity was just as important as his artistry.

The interviews with Buckley's closest friends and family members offer valuable insight into his character. These personal stories help to demystify Buckley and reveal the complexities of his personality. For example, Parker Kindred, Buckley's drummer, speaks about how Buckley's passion for music was matched only by his sensitivity to the world around him. This sensitivity, though a source of strength in his music, was also a source of personal anguish. Through these interviews, the documentary paints a portrait of a man who, despite his fame and success, was often at odds with his own emotions.

Joan Wasser's interview is particularly revealing, as she shares her experience of being romantically involved with Buckley. Her reflections on their time together highlight the deep emotional connection they shared, but they also touch on the complexities of loving an artist who was both brilliant and tortured. Wasser speaks about Buckley's capacity for love and tenderness, but also about his struggles to reconcile his emotions with the demands of his career. Her candid interview adds a layer of intimacy to the documentary, allowing the viewer to understand the man behind the songs like "Lover, You Should've Come Over."

In addition to these personal stories, the documentary also includes archival footage of Buckley, capturing moments of introspection and reflection. These rare glimpses of Buckley in his private moments allow the viewer to connect with him on a more human level. We see Buckley's warmth, his humor, and his vulnerability, traits that may not always have been apparent in his public persona. These moments help to uncover the man behind the music, showing us that Jeff Buckley was more than just a talented musician, he was a complex, emotional individual whose struggles and triumphs were deeply intertwined with his artistry.

Chapter 7: The Documentary's Cultural Relevance

It's Never Over is not just a documentary about Jeff Buckley; it's a film that explores themes of artistic struggle, emotional vulnerability, and the human condition, all of which continue to resonate with audiences today. Buckley's legacy lives on through his music, and the documentary does an excellent job of highlighting how his emotional depth and artistic integrity have impacted not only music but also the broader cultural landscape. In this chapter, we examine why *It's Never Over* remains relevant in today's cultural moment, how the film reflects larger social and cultural themes, and how Buckley's influence continues to shape modern music and culture.

Why *It's Never Over* Resonates Today

Despite Jeff Buckley's death over two decades ago, *It's Never Over* reveals how his story, and the themes explored in the film, remain profoundly relevant in today's society. In an age where authenticity and emotional transparency are increasingly celebrated, Buckley's raw vulnerability and his willingness to expose his innermost thoughts through his music feel more poignant than ever. The documentary captures the essence of Buckley's ability to connect with his audience on a deeply emotional level, and it is this emotional honesty that continues to resonate with listeners today.

The film's exploration of Buckley's internal struggles, his battle with fame, his complicated family dynamics, and his search for artistic authenticity, speaks to universal human experiences. In a world that often prioritizes surface-level appearances and instant gratification, Buckley's story offers a refreshing reminder of the value of emotional depth and artistic integrity. His reluctance to conform to the expectations of the music industry, coupled with his quest to create music that was both true to himself and relatable to his audience, makes *It's Never Over* a timeless reflection of the tension between artistic ambition and personal vulnerability.

Furthermore, the documentary touches on Buckley's legacy within the broader cultural conversation about mental health, self-doubt, and identity. In a time when these topics are being given more attention, the film serves as a reminder of the importance of addressing one's inner struggles while also celebrating the beauty that can emerge from these challenges. Buckley's vulnerability, both in his music and in his life, remains an enduring symbol of the power of emotional expression in the face of adversity.

The Film's Reflection of Larger Social and Cultural Themes

It's Never Over goes beyond telling the story of one man's life; it also reflects larger social and cultural themes that are relevant today. One of the most striking themes in the documentary is the tension between fame and authenticity. Buckley's story highlights the pressure artists face to remain true to themselves while navigating the often overwhelming demands of the music industry. His reluctance to be commodified and his struggle to maintain his artistic integrity in the face of growing fame are themes that continue to resonate with today's artists, who often face the same challenges of balancing commercial success with personal authenticity.

The documentary also touches on the complex relationships between fathers and sons, as Buckley's struggle with his father's legacy is a central part of the narrative. Mary Guibert, Buckley's mother, speaks openly about her son's internal conflict, revealing the emotional toll of living in the shadow of a legendary father. This theme of generational conflict and the search for one's own identity is something many people can relate to, particularly in today's world, where the pressure to live up to familial expectations remains a significant source of personal struggle.

Moreover, *It's Never Over* reflects the broader cultural conversation about mental health and emotional well-being. Buckley's story is not just one of artistic brilliance but also one of personal pain, emotional isolation, and the search for connection. In a time when mental health issues are increasingly recognized and discussed, the film's portrayal of Buckley's emotional struggles offers a poignant reminder of the importance of addressing mental health concerns and seeking support in times of crisis. The film doesn't shy away from exploring Buckley's battles with self-worth, anxiety, and grief, making it a powerful statement about the complexities of the human experience.

Finally, the film explores themes of love and loss, which are universal experiences that continue to resonate with audiences across generations. Buckley's music was deeply influenced by his own experiences with love, heartbreak, and the emotional turmoil that often accompanies these intense emotions. In *It's Never Over*, the documentary captures the transformative power of love, showing how Buckley's relationships, both personal and professional, shaped his music and his life. This exploration of love and loss remains relevant today, as people continue to seek meaning and connection in their relationships.

Buckley's Influence on Modern Music and Culture

One of the most enduring aspects of Jeff Buckley's legacy is his influence on modern music. Though his career was cut short, his unique sound and approach to songwriting continue to inspire artists across genres. *It's Never Over* highlights how Buckley's music has left an indelible mark on the music world, from indie rock to folk, and even alternative and electronic music.

Buckley's vocal style, characterized by its range, emotional depth, and ability to convey both fragility and power, has influenced countless singers and musicians. His ability to infuse his performances with raw emotion, as seen in songs like "Hallelujah," "Lover, You Should've Come Over," and "Last Goodbye," has set a standard for emotional honesty in contemporary music. Today's artists, including some featured in the documentary like Aimee Mann and Ben Harper, cite Buckley as an influence on their own music, particularly in how to convey vulnerability and authenticity through song.

Beyond his vocal ability, Buckley's approach to songwriting also paved the way for many modern artists who blend genres and push boundaries. His music was not easily categorized, he combined elements of folk, rock, blues, and jazz, creating a sound that was uniquely his own. This genre-blending approach has been embraced by many contemporary musicians who seek to transcend the confines of traditional genres. Artists like James Blake, Bon Iver, and even Kanye West have been influenced by Buckley's ability to create music that is deeply personal, emotionally complex, and sonically innovative.

Moreover, Buckley's legacy is felt in the way his music continues to inspire new generations of fans. *It's Never Over* highlights the way Buckley's songs have become anthems for people experiencing heartbreak, longing, and loss. His music remains a cultural touchstone for those seeking emotional catharsis through music, and his songs continue to be covered by artists and featured in films and TV shows, further cementing his place in modern culture.

Buckley's influence also extends to the way we view the artist's role in society. He remains a symbol of the tortured artist, someone who poured their soul into their work, even at the expense of their own emotional well-being. In a world where the pressure to succeed is immense, and where the intersection of fame and personal identity continues to be a point of contention, Buckley's story is a reminder of the cost of artistic genius and the importance of staying true to oneself.

Chapter 8: Audience Reception and Critical Response

It's Never Over has been a significant cultural moment, offering not only a tribute to Jeff Buckley's legacy but also a reflection on the emotional depth and artistry that continues to influence generations. Upon its debut, the documentary quickly sparked intense discussions among critics and audiences alike. From its world premiere at the Sundance Film Festival to its wide-reaching impact on music lovers and filmgoers, *It's Never Over* has garnered attention for its poignant storytelling, intimate approach, and insightful portrayal of an artist whose influence transcends time. This chapter delves into how the film was received at Sundance 2025, examines the critical reviews and public reactions, and shares what viewers have said about the documentary.

How the Film Was Received at Sundance 2025

The premiere of *It's Never Over* at the 2025 Sundance Film Festival marked a major milestone for the documentary. Sundance, renowned for showcasing some of the best independent films, provided the perfect stage for a project as emotionally compelling and culturally relevant as this one. The documentary immediately captured the attention of festivalgoers, many of whom were Buckley fans or musicians influenced by his work.

At Sundance, the film received an overwhelmingly positive response for its raw and intimate portrayal of Jeff Buckley's life. Audiences were deeply moved by the way the documentary blended personal interviews, archival footage, and powerful live performances. Amy Berg's direction was praised for capturing the essence of Buckley without sensationalizing his struggles or romanticizing his genius. The filmmakers' ability to balance the beauty of Buckley's music with the complexity of his personal life was widely appreciated.

Mary Guibert, Buckley's mother, was present at the Sundance screening, and her involvement in the documentary added a level of authenticity and emotional weight to the film. The heartfelt reflections shared by Guibert, along with those from Buckley's bandmates, Aimee Mann, Ben Harper, and others, left a lasting impact on festival attendees. Guibert's candidness about her son's life and her role in preserving his legacy resonated deeply with the audience, helping them to connect not just with the music but with the man behind it.

Critics and viewers at Sundance were particularly impressed by the emotional depth of the film. Many praised its ability to avoid typical biographical clichés and instead present a nuanced and empathetic portrayal of Buckley. The documentary's approach was seen as a respectful and thoughtful exploration of the artist's life and legacy, avoiding the sensationalism that often surrounds the stories of rock stars.

Critical Reviews and Public Reactions

Following its premiere at Sundance, *It's Never Over* received widespread acclaim from critics, who praised its emotional honesty and cinematic execution. Reviewers highlighted the film's ability to capture not only the artistic brilliance of Jeff Buckley but also the personal struggles that shaped his music.

Many critics noted how the documentary excelled in balancing the portrayal of Buckley's public success with his private struggles. The film's focus on Buckley's emotional and psychological challenges was praised for its authenticity. Critics pointed out how the documentary allows viewers to witness Buckley's vulnerabilities, his battle with fame, his complex relationship with his father's legacy, and his internal conflict with self-doubt and identity. These themes are explored in depth through interviews with Mary Guibert, as well as Buckley's bandmates, Aimee Mann, and Ben Harper, who provided candid and heartfelt insights into Buckley's personal and professional life.

The cinematography and music were also frequently mentioned in reviews, with many critics commending the way the film used Buckley's own music to illuminate key moments in his life. The inclusion of his live performances, particularly his rendition of "Hallelujah," was highlighted as one of the most powerful aspects of the film. Critics noted how the use of these performances in the documentary not only celebrated Buckley's artistry but also underscored the emotional complexity of his character.

While the film received almost universal praise, a few critics mentioned that the documentary could have benefited from even deeper exploration into Buckley's music, particularly his songwriting process and the broader influence of *Grace*. Nonetheless, most agreed that the film did an excellent job of presenting a multifaceted portrait of Buckley, one that was both intimate and reflective.

Public reactions to *It's Never Over* were overwhelmingly positive as well. Fans of Buckley praised the film for providing a deeper understanding of the man behind the music. Social media platforms and online forums were abuzz with discussions about the film, with many viewers expressing how deeply the documentary moved them. Fans noted that *It's Never Over* helped them connect with Buckley's music on a more personal level, offering new insights into the emotional depth of his work.

What Viewers Are Saying About *It's Never Over*

Since its release, viewers have shared their thoughts on *It's Never Over*, expressing how the documentary has impacted them both as fans of Jeff Buckley and as people who appreciate the emotional power of music. Many viewers have mentioned how the film gave them a more nuanced understanding of Buckley's life and artistry. They shared that the documentary's portrayal of Buckley's struggles with fame, family, and personal identity made his music feel even more meaningful.

One common sentiment among viewers is how *It's Never Over* makes them feel closer to Buckley. By showcasing not only his musical genius but also his vulnerabilities, the film invites audiences to see Buckley as a human being, not just as an enigmatic artist. Comments on social media and fan websites often reflect how the documentary made viewers reflect on their own personal experiences with love, loss, and emotional struggle, showing how Buckley's music transcends time and connects with people on a deeply personal level.

Many viewers also appreciated the candid interviews with those closest to Buckley, such as Mary Guibert, Parker Kindred, and Joan Wasser. These interviews allowed audiences to see a side of Buckley that was rarely visible in public. Fans felt that the documentary provided them with a more complete picture of who Buckley was, both as an artist and as a person. Several viewers mentioned that hearing Guibert talk about her son's life and legacy made them feel as though they had gained a deeper, more intimate understanding of his character and motivations.

Aimee Mann's contribution to the documentary, where she reflects on the way Buckley's music influenced her own, resonated with many viewers. Fans of both Buckley and Mann were particularly moved by the way Mann spoke about the emotional connection she shared with Buckley, despite their differing musical styles. Many viewers commented on how her reflections brought a new level of appreciation for both artists' work.

Some fans, especially those who had discovered Buckley's music posthumously, expressed gratitude for the film's ability to highlight his lasting impact on music. They shared that *It's Never Over* provided them with a new lens through which to appreciate Buckley's music, which had already become a source of solace and inspiration for many. The documentary made them realize how Buckley's work continues to inspire musicians, songwriters, and fans across the globe.

Chapter 9: Impact and Legacy – What the Film Leaves Behind

It's Never Over does more than just chronicle the life of Jeff Buckley; it preserves his legacy and ensures that his influence will continue to echo through generations to come. This chapter explores the lasting impact of the documentary, examining how it plays a crucial role in preserving Buckley's memory, how documentaries like this shape musical legacies, and how the film continues to inspire both musicians and fans today.

Preserving Jeff Buckley's Memory Through Film

The legacy of Jeff Buckley is one that has been carefully cultivated by his family, collaborators, and fans since his tragic death in 1997. Yet, his memory and artistic contributions have often been relegated to the realm of music lovers and those familiar with *Grace*. *It's Never Over* ensures that Buckley's legacy reaches a wider audience by capturing the essence of the man behind the music. The documentary is not only a tribute to his artistry but also an effort to preserve the emotional and personal aspects of his life that might otherwise have been lost.

Mary Guibert, Buckley's mother, plays a crucial role in the preservation of his memory. Her involvement in the documentary is deeply personal, offering insights into Buckley's character, struggles, and growth as an artist. Through her reflections, viewers gain an understanding of the delicate balance she had to strike as a mother, nurturing his talents while also protecting his privacy. Guibert's contributions are essential in ensuring that Buckley's life is seen through the eyes of those who truly understood him.

The documentary offers a glimpse into the quieter, more intimate moments of Buckley's life that were rarely captured by the media or seen by the public. By presenting archival footage, rare live performances, and heartfelt interviews with those closest to him, such as his bandmates Michael Tighe and Parker Kindred, as well as romantic partners like Joan Wasser, the film builds a multi-faceted portrait of an artist whose life, though brief, was rich with emotional depth. This is not just a film for Buckley's fans; it's a gift to future generations who will now have access to a more complete understanding of the man whose music continues to speak to the human experience.

In this way, *It's Never Over* becomes a timeless tool for preserving Buckley's memory. By capturing the essence of his life and legacy, the documentary ensures that his influence will be felt long after the final note of *Grace* fades. It cements his place not only in music history but also in the cultural consciousness as an artist who dared to be vulnerable, open, and honest through his work.

The Role of Documentaries in Shaping Musical Legacies

Documentaries have long played a vital role in shaping and preserving the legacies of musicians, and *It's Never Over* is no exception. While Buckley's music continues to live on through albums like *Grace*, it's often the personal stories and the behind-the-scenes moments that make an artist's legacy endure. Through documentaries like *It's Never Over*, audiences gain deeper access to the artist's journey, struggles, and triumphs, which ultimately shapes how the world remembers them.

Amy Berg's direction of *It's Never Over* exemplifies how a well-crafted documentary can serve as both a historical record and an emotional tribute. The documentary format allows for a deeper exploration of Jeff Buckley's life than a traditional biography or interview could offer. By focusing on both his public persona and his private struggles, the film highlights the complexity of Buckley's character. It's this multi-dimensional view that creates a lasting and authentic legacy, ensuring that his contributions to music are not forgotten and that future generations can experience his work in a more personal way.

It's Never Over also plays a role in amplifying the stories of those who were close to Buckley and who contributed to his musical journey. The voices of his mother, Mary Guibert, as well as musicians like Aimee Mann and Ben Harper, provide additional layers of depth to the film, helping to contextualize Buckley's music in the broader history of rock and indie music. By capturing these voices and perspectives, the film solidifies its place as an integral part of Buckley's legacy.

Moreover, this documentary demonstrates the power of storytelling in preserving a musical legacy. While Buckley's albums may continue to inspire, *It's Never Over* ensures that the story of how those albums came to be, and the emotional struggles behind their creation, will remain a vital part of his narrative. It's through these stories that an artist's legacy is truly shaped, and this documentary serves as a crucial piece in ensuring that Buckley's influence continues to grow.

How the Film Inspires the Next Generation of Musicians and Fans

One of the most significant impacts of *It's Never Over* is the way it inspires both aspiring musicians and the fans who continue to find solace in Buckley's music. Through the documentary, young artists can see not only the brilliance of Buckley's sound but also the emotional courage it took for him to share his vulnerability with the world. The film reveals that Buckley's greatest strength was his ability to channel his internal struggles into his art. This message resonates deeply with today's musicians, who are often faced with the same challenges of authenticity, self-doubt, and the pressure to succeed.

The film's exploration of Buckley's artistic process and his commitment to creating music that was true to himself is a source of inspiration for new generations of musicians. Buckley's ability to blend genres, from rock to jazz to folk, has become a model for artists seeking to push the boundaries of musical genres and express their own unique voices. His fearlessness in exposing his vulnerability through songs like "Lover, You Should've Come Over" and his iconic cover of "Hallelujah" encourages musicians to embrace their own emotional depth and take risks in their work.

For fans, *It's Never Over* serves as a powerful reminder of the healing power of music. Buckley's songs, which often deal with themes of love, heartbreak, and existential questioning, continue to resonate with people across the globe. Many viewers of the documentary have shared how Buckley's music helped them navigate their own personal struggles, and the film amplifies this emotional connection by showing how Buckley's life was intertwined with the very themes he explored in his music.

The documentary also introduces Buckley's story to a new generation of listeners who may not have experienced his music during his lifetime. For younger fans discovering Buckley's work for the first time, *It's Never Over* is a crucial bridge between his music and his personal story. By bringing attention to the emotional depth of Buckley's life, the documentary creates a deeper connection between his songs and the fans who continue to find meaning in them. This new audience is exposed to the layers of his artistry, his vulnerability, his strength, and the beauty he created in the face of personal turmoil.

Moreover, *It's Never Over* is an essential piece for the continuing conversation about the intersection of mental health and artistry. Buckley's willingness to confront his inner struggles through music serves as an example for the next generation of musicians, showing that it is possible to channel personal pain into something beautiful and universally relatable. The film's honest portrayal of Buckley's battle with self-doubt and fame helps normalize these experiences, empowering aspiring artists to use their own struggles as fuel for their creative expression.

Chapter 10: Final Thoughts – Reflecting on the Documentary and its Significance

As the final chapter of *It's Never Over* unfolds, we are left with a powerful reflection on the life and legacy of Jeff Buckley. His story, told through the lens of Amy Berg's sensitive and thoughtful documentary, serves not only as a reminder of the fleeting nature of fame but also as a testament to the enduring power of artistic expression. This chapter takes a moment to pause and reflect on the lasting significance of both the documentary and Buckley's legacy, considering his enduring appeal, the film's success in capturing his essence, and why *It's Never Over* resonates deeply with music lovers and film buffs alike.

The Enduring Appeal of Jeff Buckley

Jeff Buckley's appeal lies not only in his exceptional musical talent but in his ability to speak directly to the emotions of his listeners. His music, particularly the album *Grace*, carries an emotional weight that transcends time. His voice, a mix of ethereal fragility and soaring power, conveys emotions that many musicians can only hope to evoke. His ability to express profound vulnerability through his songs has made him a unique figure in music history. And although he passed away far too young, Buckley's impact on both the music industry and the hearts of listeners has continued to grow in the years since his death.

It's Never Over shines a spotlight on the reasons why Buckley's appeal is still so strong, more than two decades after his passing. The film illustrates not just his musical brilliance but the personal qualities that made him so relatable, his emotional complexity, his sensitivity, and his search for artistic purity. These are qualities that continue to resonate with fans, whether they discovered his music at the time of its release or later on in life.

Buckley's songs are timeless because they deal with universal themes: love, longing, loss, and personal growth. His struggles, both emotional and professional, are ones that many can relate to. His voice, which still carries the weight of his raw emotion, continues to be a source of solace for those experiencing heartbreak or searching for meaning in their lives. The documentary highlights how Buckley's music speaks to this raw human experience, making his work more relevant than ever.

In *It's Never Over*, his mother, Mary Guibert, reflects on her son's desire to be understood and his reluctance to be defined by anyone, even his own family legacy. She offers a deeply personal glimpse into the man who would become the icon that many mourn today. This exploration of Buckley's humanity is one of the reasons why his appeal remains so strong; he represents the artist who poured his heart into his music and, in doing so, created a timeless connection with those who listened.

Analyzing the Documentary's Success in Capturing His Spirit

It's Never Over succeeds not only as a historical account of Jeff Buckley's life but also in capturing the very spirit of who he was as an artist. Amy Berg's direction ensures that the documentary is not just a chronology of Buckley's career but a deep dive into his personal experiences, emotions, and the driving force behind his music. The film's success lies in its ability to balance the universal appeal of Buckley's music with the deeply intimate and often painful aspects of his life.

One of the key successes of the documentary is its ability to weave together archival footage of Buckley's performances with the reflective interviews of those closest to him. The juxtaposition of these elements allows the audience to not only hear Buckley's music but also understand the emotional landscape from which it came. We see the raw energy of his performances, where his vulnerability becomes palpable. His iconic rendition of "Hallelujah," as shown in the film, becomes a powerful emblem of Buckley's ability to channel his personal struggles into something universally beautiful.

The documentary's use of personal interviews with Mary Guibert, Aimee Mann, Michael Tighe, Ben Harper, and others is equally important in capturing Buckley's spirit. Guibert, in particular, gives the audience a sense of what it was like to raise a child who would later become a legendary figure in music. Her reflections, combined with those of Buckley's bandmates and romantic partners, paint a picture of a man who was both deeply caring and deeply conflicted. The candidness of these interviews adds depth to the documentary, making Buckley feel more human and relatable. These voices help bridge the gap between Buckley the icon and Buckley the person, showing how the two were inseparably linked.

Berg's careful editing and pacing also contribute to the film's success. The emotional moments are allowed to breathe, giving the viewer the time to fully absorb the weight of Buckley's life and struggles. There is no rush to move through Buckley's story; rather, the film takes its time, allowing moments of reflection to sink in. This unhurried approach mirrors Buckley's own way of creating music, each note, each word, deeply considered and deliberate.

Ultimately, the documentary succeeds in capturing the essence of Buckley's spirit. Through his music, his words, and the reflections of those who knew him, *It's Never Over* makes clear that Buckley's greatest legacy is not just in the songs he recorded but in the emotional resonance those songs continue to have with people.

Conclusion: Why *It's Never Over* Matters for Music Lovers and Film Buffs Alike

It's Never Over is a film that matters for both music lovers and film buffs because it transcends the boundaries of the typical music documentary. For music lovers, it offers an in-depth look at the genius of Jeff Buckley, his process, his emotional depth, and the artistry that went into creating his unforgettable songs. The documentary delves into Buckley's life and music in a way that allows viewers to understand not just his achievements but also the personal battles he faced in his brief time on earth. Through this, it offers a deeper connection to the music and a greater appreciation for Buckley's legacy.

For film buffs, *It's Never Over* is an excellent example of how a documentary can be more than just a biographical recounting of an artist's life. It is a work of cinematic art that blends visuals, music, and interviews to create a cohesive and emotionally resonant narrative. The film is a testament to the power of storytelling and the importance of capturing the emotional essence of a person's life. Director Amy Berg's careful approach to the material ensures that the documentary isn't just about the past, it's a reflection on the enduring power of art, the struggles behind it, and the cultural impact of Jeff Buckley's music.

It's Never Over matters because it reminds us that great art does not simply live on in records or performances, it lives in the way it touches the hearts of those who experience it. The documentary captures the universal themes of love, loss, and longing that are woven into Buckley's music, and through it, we see that his legacy will never truly end. His music continues to inspire and connect people, and *It's Never Over* ensures that his story will never be forgotten. Whether you are a long-time fan or new to his music, the film offers a way to understand and appreciate the depth of his artistry, making it an essential piece for music lovers and film buffs alike.

Manufactured by Amazon.ca
Acheson, AB